FLIGHT

FLYING ANIMALS

June Loves

This edition first published in 2002 in the United States of America by Chelsea House Publishers, a subsidiary of Haights Cross Communications

Chelsea House Publishers
1974 Sproul Road, Suite 400
Broomall, PA 19008-0914

The Chelsea House world wide web address is www.chelseahouse.com

Library of Congress Cataloging-in-Publication Data Applied for.
ISBN 0-7910-6561-8

First published in 2000 by
Macmillan Education Australia Pty Ltd
627 Chapel Street, South Yarra, Australia, 3141

Text copyright © June Loves 2000

Edited by Lara Whitehead
Text design by if Design
Cover design by if Design
Page layout by if Design/Raul Diche
Illustrations by Lorenzo Lucia
Printed in Hong Kong

Acknowledgements
The author and the publisher are grateful to the following for permission to reproduce copyright material:

Cover: Fischer's Lovebird (center), courtesy of Jean-Michael Labat/AUSCAPE; Tabanid fly (background), courtesy of C. Andrew Henley/ AUSCAPE.

Photographs courtesy of: Nicholas Birks/AUSCAPE, pp. 14–5; John Cancalosi/AUSCAPE, p. 4; Stephen Dalton-OSF/AUSCAPE, pp. 24–5; Jean-Paul Ferrero/AUSCAPE, pp. 2 (right), 11 (right), 15 (right), 17, 19, 24 (bottom left); Ferrero-Labat/AUSCAPE, pp. 3 (bottom), 28–9; Francois Gohier/AUSCAPE, p. 5 (bottom right); C. Andrew Henley/AUSCAPE, pp. 2–3 (background), 12–3, 13 (bottom left), 30–1 (background), 32; Richard Herrmann-OSF/AUSCAPE, p. 18; M.P. Kahl/AUSCAPE, p. 29 (bottom); Jean-Michel Labat/AUSCAPE, pp. 20–1; Joe McDonald/AUSCAPE, pp. 26–7; Alastair Shay/AUSCAPE, p. 10; Anne & Jacques Six/AUSCAPE, p. 7 (top); Albert Visage/AUSCAPE, p. 23 (top); Australian Picture Library/Orion Press International, p. 16; International Photographic Library, p. 13 (bottom right); The Photo Library/Hulton Deutsch, p. 30; Silkstone/Southern Images SA, pp. 6, 7 (bottom), 9, 11 (left).

While every care has been taken to trace and acknowledge copyright the publishers tender their apologies for any accidental infringement where copyright has proved untraceable.

Contents

Prehistoric flyers

THE FIRST ANIMALS BEGAN to fly about 400 million years ago. Through **evolution** they developed special features such as skin flaps to help them fly. For many animals, these skin flaps later evolved into wings.

PREHISTORIC INSECTS

Insects were the first flying animals. Giant dragonflies evolved about 350 million years ago, long before the dinosaurs walked on the earth. Some prehistoric dragonflies had **wingspans** of up to one meter (3.28 feet). Many other flying insects, similar to those we know today, evolved during the next 150 million years. Although dinosaurs have become extinct, insects have thrived.

A dragonfly fossil.

Prehistoric beetles

In prehistoric times, beetles had two pairs of wings. Over millions of years, the front pair of wings have changed into hard, close-fitting covers that protect the flying wings underneath. All beetles used to be flying insects. Many now live on the ground and cannot fly.

GLIDING REPTILES

About 200 million years ago, the first gliding reptiles appeared. The longisquama had tall crests along its back that could have opened up like wings. It used these to glide through the air but was not able to flap its wings for true flying.

Rhamphorthyncus also lived about 200 million years ago. It was one type of gliding reptile and had a long tail that probably acted like a rudder for steering in the air.

FLYING REPTILES

Pterosaurs

Pterosaurs, giant winged lizards, evolved from the gliding reptiles. Pterosaurs flew in the air at the same time as dinosaurs lived on the ground. Scientists used to think that pterosaurs could only glide. They now believe that many could fly well. Their wings were made of skin and they had light bones, which made it easier for them to fly.

A pterosaur.

Archaeopteryx

The archaeopteryx lived 150 million years ago. It was the first feathered creature known to have existed. The archaeopteryx could glide and fly. It had a mouth full of teeth, bird-like wings and legs, and a tail like a lizard. A fossilized archaeopteryx was found in Germany in 1860 and more fossilized remains have been discovered since then.

About 65 million years ago, the dinosaurs died out, along with gliding, flying and swimming reptiles. Scientists are not certain of the reasons for this.

This fossil of an archaeopteryx shows the details of the wings and feathers.

 Flying Fact

The quetzalocoatlus, a pterosaur, was the largest flying animal ever to exist. It had a wingspan of 12 meters (39.4 feet), which is wider than most hang-gliders.

Insects

FLYING IS IMPORTANT TO many insects' survival. It is an excellent way to travel to find food. It also allows many insects to escape from danger and to find mates. Most insects have wings and can fly at some stage in their life cycles. Today there are more insects that fly than any other animal.

INSECTS' WINGS

Insects' wings do not contain bone or muscle. They are flat and covered with tiny hairs or scales. Tiny, tough veins stiffen and support the wings. Each **species** of insect has a different pattern of veins on its wings. Scientists use these different patterns to tell one species of insect from another.

HOW INSECTS FLY

Muscles in the thorax provide power for insects' wings. These muscles either flap the wings directly or make the thorax move, which causes the wings to flap. Different kinds of insects beat their wings at different speeds. The faster the wings beat, the higher the buzzing sound.

Insects control their flight by beating their wings in complicated patterns. Their wings make swirling currents of air that provide **lift** and **thrust** for movement through the air.

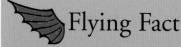

Flying Fact

Some insects such as locusts and midges gather and fly in swarms. A swarm can contain a few dozen insects or billions of them.

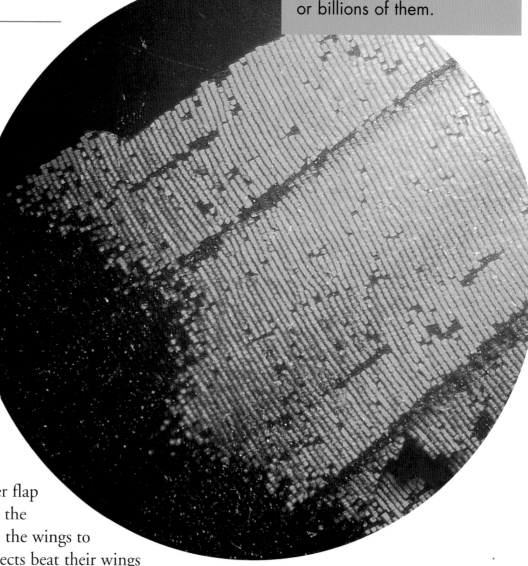

Close-up of the scales on a butterfly's wing.

HONEYBEES

A worker honeybee is a typical flying insect. It has two pairs of wings. Worker honeybees, like all insects, have a body that is divided into three parts: the head, thorax and abdomen.

Antennae

Head

Abdomen—contains the digestive system, organs for reproduction and the sting organs

Mouth parts— used to gather food and guide it into the insect's mouth

Eyes—an adult insect has **compound eyes**

Thorax—three pairs of legs and two pairs of wings are attached to the thorax

A worker bee.

Exoskeleton—hard, outer covering of the body

Flying is a fast and effective way of moving from flower to flower for honeybees, but it uses lots of energy. Honeybees refuel with the nectar from plants, which gives them more energy.

A honeybee's wings

The wings of a honeybee, like all insects, are made of chitin. This is the same hard, plastic-like substance that makes the exoskeleton of an insect. The larger front wings are joined to the smaller back wings by a row of hooks. The two pairs of wings beat together as the honeybee travels through the air.

DRAGONFLIES

DRAGONFLIES ARE STRONG, powerful flyers, even though their wings look light and fragile. Dragonflies can hover, fly backwards and change direction at high speeds.

The adult dragonfly lives in air but the young dragonfly develops under water. Most dragonflies live near rivers, swamps and ponds where they hunt other insects such as small flies and mosquitoes.

Growing wings

A dragonfly only changes shape slightly as it develops from a young insect to an adult. The young dragonfly, called a nymph, does not have wings, only wing buds. Nymphs are a different color from the adult, eat different food and live in the water.

Moulting

The young nymph molts by shedding its skin. Each time it grows bigger the wing buds also grow bigger.

Life cycle of a dragonfly

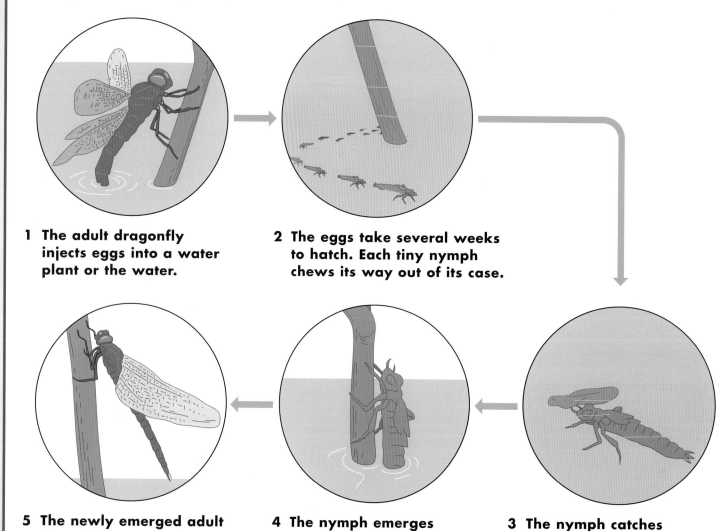

1 The adult dragonfly injects eggs into a water plant or the water.

2 The eggs take several weeks to hatch. Each tiny nymph chews its way out of its case.

5 The newly emerged adult dragonfly rests in the sun while its wings expand and dry before it can fly off.

4 The nymph emerges from the water when it is ready to molt for the last time.

3 The nymph catches tadpoles, worms and even small fish. They live in water for up to five years.

How a dragonfly flies

Most insects flap their wings together but a dragonfly uses its two pairs of wings separately. The front and back wings beat in opposite directions. As the dragonfly beats its front wings down, the air is stirred up and passes over the back wings, creating lift. With each beat, the wings push the air down and back. This moves the dragonfly up and forward. An **articulated** tail helps the dragonfly steer.

Meals on the wing

Adult dragonflies use their powerful eyesight and excellent flying skills to attack other insects in the air. They swoop down over water and catch other insects for food with their long legs.

MOTHS AND BUTTERFLIES

Moths and butterflies can be graceful flyers. Butterflies fly in the daytime but moths fly mostly at night or in the early morning. During the day, they stay hidden in leaves or trees.

Wing patterns

Moths' and butterflies' wings are many different colors and are decorated with different patterns. The powdery scales on their wings overlap to make the colors and patterns. Butterflies' wings are usually bright and attractive colors; moths usually have dull-colored wings.

METAMORPHOSIS

Moths and butterflies do not start life as flying insects with wings. They begin life as an egg and their bodies go through a huge change called **metamorphosis**.

LIFE CYCLE OF A BUTTERFLY

1 Egg—the adult butterfly lays eggs on leaves.

2 Caterpillar—the egg hatches into a caterpillar called the larva. The larva feeds on plants and grows until it changes into a pupa.

3 **Pupa**—the body of the butterfly develops inside the pupa. It can also be called a chrysalis.

4 Butterfly—an adult butterfly emerges from the pupa with damp and crumpled wings. It spreads it wings to dry and harden and then flies off to find a mate. The life cycle continues again.

The bright colors and designs of a butterfly's wings make it easy to identify species of butterflies. Swallowtail butterflies get their name from the long tails on each back wing.

Long-distance fliers

Some insects travel for great distances in search of food and warmth. Dragonflies, locusts and moths often migrate. In spring, the North American monarch butterfly migrates more than 2,400 kilometers (1,491 miles) across North America each year.

Butterflies rest with their wings together, standing straight up from their body. They beat their wings to provide lift and propel themselves through the air.

How moths and butterflies fly

Moths and butterflies have two pairs of wings. The front and back wings on each side work together like one wing. Butterflies and moths can hover and maneuver in the air.

Defence

Many butterflies and moths have wonderful eye patterns on their wings. When they are threatened, they suddenly open up their wings to display two huge eyes. This can threaten enemies and frighten them away.

Bogong moths

Bogong moths migrate in the spring. During the hot, dry summer of southeastern Australia, the moths hibernate in caves and cracks in rocks high in the mountains. In the autumn they fly down to the lowlands to lay their eggs. Some keep flying and are lost in the sea.

FLIES

Flies only have one pair of wings but fly with great speed and **agility**. There are over 120,000 known species of flies, including midges, mosquitoes and brightly colored hover flies. They all begin life as eggs.

Landing upside down

Flies can land upside down on the ceiling but they hit front feet first. Scientists use high-speed cameras to watch this action because the process only takes a fraction of a second.

When a fly is about to land it flies right side up, but lifts its front legs above its body. The pads on the front legs secrete a sticky fluid and the claws on its front feet catch hold of the ceiling. The fly's body then flips upside down. Its other four legs make contact with the surface covered with the sticky fluid. This fastens it securely to the ceiling.

Hover flies

Hover flies are also expert fliers. They are one of the few insects that are able to hover for long periods of time. They can fly in any direction, forward, backward and sideways, as well as hover.

Halters are special balancing organs that act as stabilizers and rotate rapidly when flies are flying. They are tiny ball-and-stick structures behind the wings.

BEETLES

There are more species of beetle in the world than any other kind of animal. Scientists believe there are more than 400,000 different kinds of beetles and more are being discovered each year.

Beetles have many different shapes, sizes and colors but all beetles have four wings. The front wings are hard and tough and fit over the back wings like a case. These hard outer wings are called elytra. They protect the fragile wings that are actually used for flying.

Flying Fact

A house fly averages a speed of seven kilometers (4.3 miles) per hour and beats its wings 200 times per second.

A mosquito averages a speed of 1.5 kilometers (one mile) per hour and beats its wing 600 times per second.

A ladybird is often called a 'ladybug'. It is not a bug but belongs to a group of insects called beetles.

How beetles fly

A ladybird is a type of beetle. When it is on the ground, its back wings are normally packed away under its front wings.

Before a ladybird can fly, the front wings must swing outwards so the back wings can unfold. The front wings provide lift, which helps the ladybird stay in the air. When the back wings are beating fast enough to reach flying speed, the ladybird takes off.

The ladybird's hard front-wing cases protect its back wings when it is not flying.

As it takes off, the front wings of a ladybird swing out and away from the back wings.

Bats

BATS ARE THE ONLY mammals that can fly. Most bats are nocturnal animals. By day, bats sleep upside down in **roosts**. They hang by their clawed back feet, their wings wrapped around them.

At night, bats fly out to find food. Most bats eat insects and catch moths and other insects in the air at night. Other bats feed on fruit, nectar, small mammals and fish.

HOW BATS FLY

Bats have powerful muscles in their chest that are used to flap their wings. During flight the bat's wings are supported by long, thin arm and finger bones. The wings push down to create lift. Bats can twist and turn in the air as they chase insects for food.

BATS' WINGS

Bats' wings are made of thin skin that is stretched between their arm and finger bones. Only the thumb is free. This is used as a claw when clambering and holding. The skin stretches between the fingers and down the side of the body to the bat's hind legs.

Wings stretch between the forearm and finger bones

Many bones in the wing

Echo location

Bats have an excellent **navigation** system that they use when they are flying in the dark. This is called 'echo location'. As bats fly in the dark, they make a series of high-pitched squeaks and clicks, which humans cannot hear. As the sounds hit objects such as a tree or insect, echoes or sound waves are reflected back to the bat. The bat interprets these sounds and can build up a picture of its surroundings, determining the size and location of an object very quickly.

The ghost bat is also called the false vampire bat.

YOUNG BATS

Young bats are born helpless and almost hairless but develop quickly. They are left in nursery roosts while parents fly off to find food. After three to ten days, their eyes open and within the first week their coats begin to grow. They can soon walk and climb. The smaller bats can fly after three to five weeks.

THE LARGEST BAT

Fruit bats are the largest bats. They measure more than two meters (6.7 feet) from wingtip to wingtip but weigh only one kilogram (2.2 pounds). They fly out at dawn and dusk to feed on fruit, flowers and leaves. At night they hang upside down in trees with their wings wrapped around them.

Flying Fact

The first bat existed about 50 million years ago.

A Christmas Island fruit bat.

Flying animals

SOME ANIMALS, such as flying squirrels, flying fish and flying frogs, are called flying animals but they do not truly fly. They glide through the air using thin folds of skin, which are not true wings. Some of these animals can steer themselves in the air but they cannot keep themselves flying.

GLIDING MAMMALS

There are three unrelated groups of mammals that can glide through the air. They are flying squirrels, flying lemurs and phalangers.

Flying squirrels

The most common gliding mammal is the flying squirrel. It is found in North America, Europe and Asia and two groups are found in Africa. They look like, and live similar lives to, the true squirrels.

A flying squirrel has folds of thin skin between the front and back legs. They start their flight high up in a tree just as a hang-glider launches from a cliff-top. The squirrels spring into space, opening their legs to spread the skin, which catches the air like a wing. They can glide in this way from tree to tree. Larger species can glide over 100 meters (328 feet).

Flying lemurs

The colugo, or flying lemur, can easily glide 100 meters (328 feet) or more between trees. They are found in the Philippines, Indonesia, Malaysia and southern China. Flying lemurs are about the size of a cat. They have elaborate folds of skin to help them glide. The skin extends to link the whole of the tail and toes. When they glide from tree to tree they look like small kites.

This white-cheeked giant flying squirrel's long bushy tail keeps it stable in flight.

Flying phalangers

Flying phalangers are often knows as flying possums, and more usually as gliders. They are marsupials, or pouched animals, and are only found in eastern Australia, Tasmania and New Guinea. They do not fly, but glide for considerable distances through the air. They have long bushy tails and their gliding surface is similar to that of the flying squirrels. Flying phalangers are common animals, but because they are nocturnal, they are rarely seen.

Flying Fact

Flying foxes are not true foxes. They are a large kind of bat with a face like a fox and are really fruit bats.

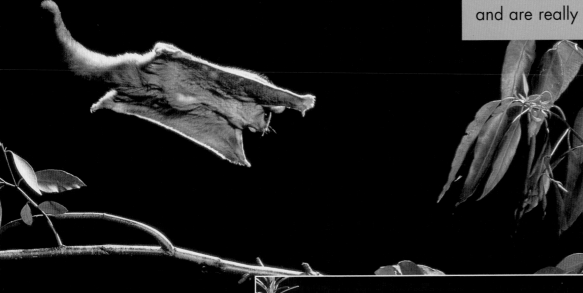

Sugar gliders are small animals and weigh 130 grams (4.6 ounces) or less.

Sugar gliders

Sugar gliders got their name because they like to eat the sugar-rich nectar of flowers. They also eat insects. They have limited control of their flight, and some species can bank and change direction after take-off.

Feather-tail gliders can travel up to 20 meters (65.6 feet) in one glide.

Feather-tail gliders

There are two **species** of feather-tail gliders. One is found in Australia and the other in New Guinea. They are the size of a mouse and live on flower nectar and insects. Their feather-like tails are used to steer and brake as they glide through the air and anchor themselves on trees.

OTHER FLYING ANIMALS

Flying frogs

Flying frogs have enormous webbed feet. Their feet and toes are connected by thin skin. They use their feet as parachutes when they glide through the air in search of insects.

To begin their flight, flying frogs climb up something tall. Sticky pads on their toes help them to climb. Some flying frogs jump from a height of 40 meters (131 feet). Then they take a huge leap, and stretch their legs outward. The membranes between their toes act like parachutes and help them land. By altering the shape of their feet, they control their flight. They glide along quickly, covering about 30 meters (98 feet) in only eight seconds.

Flying fish

Flying fish do not really fly but glide above the surface of the water to escape their enemies. Flying fish have rigid wing-like fins and an uneven forked tail. They use their tails to give them thrust as they burst from the water and spread their fins to glide across the water. Some flying fish can glide across the water surface at about 16 kilometers (10 miles) per hour. The longest recorded flight for a flying fish lasted 90 seconds and covered more than one kilometer (0.6 mile).

There are about 40 species of flying fish found in warm ocean waters around the world.

Flying lizards are sometimes called flying dragons.

Flying snakes

Three kinds of flying snakes live in trees and are found in southern Asia. They are able to glide for short distances through the air from tree to tree. By spreading their ribs they flatten their bodies to act as a kind of parachute. Flying snakes are active by day and eat rodents, bats, birds and lizards.

Flying lizards

Flying lizards, sometimes called flying dragons, have folds of scaly skin along each side of their body. These are supported by spines hinged to the ribs. When danger threatens, the spines stick out, extending the folds of skin and allowing the lizard to glide away. Flying lizards can glide from tree to tree for up to six meters (19.7 feet).

Birds—the expert fliers

BIRDS ARE THE EXPERT FLIERS of the animal world. They are the only feathered animals and can fly further and faster than any other animal. Birds have a streamlined shape and light weight, which makes them perfectly adapted for flight. Their wings are perfectly designed to allow them to fly, soar, glide and hover in the air.

A Fischer's lovebird.

A lightweight beak is well suited to help the bird eat

Excellent eyesight allows a bird to spot food at long distances and when flying at high speeds

A large heart beats ten to fifteen times each second. It circulates blood containing oxygen and food needed for flying

Powerful chest muscles control wing flapping and less strong back muscles pull the wings up

STREAMLINED BODY SHAPE

Flying birds differ in size but they have generally similar shapes. Some birds fly through the air at a greater speed than others. They have a more streamlined shape. This cuts down air resistance, or drag, and they can glide easily through the air.

Airfoil-shaped wings provides lift to keep the bird in the air

Wing feathers overlap to give a wide, flat, airtight surface, which is good for flying

Body feathers reduce air resistance and are effective insulators

A light, yet strong, body to take the stresses of taking off and landing

The tail can alter shape and position for extra lift, braking and steering

Flying Fact

Some birds cannot fly. The world's largest bird, the North African ostrich, weighs about 155 kilograms (342 pounds) and is too heavy to fly.

A BIRD'S SKELETON

A bird's skeleton is extremely strong but also very light. A bird's large bones are hollow tubes rather than solid structures. Internal **cross-bracing** strengthens them.

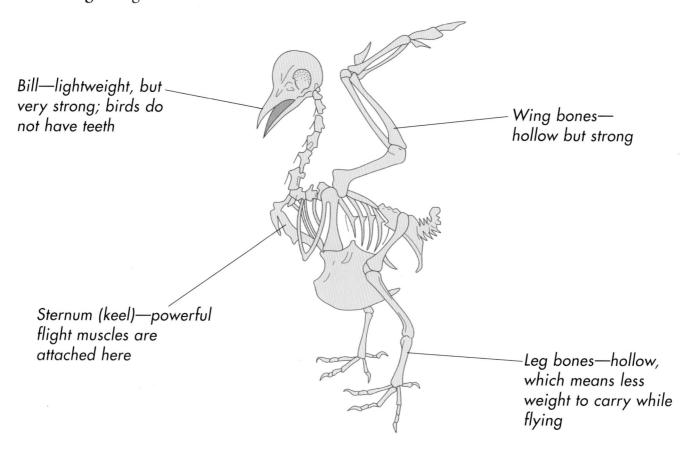

Bill—lightweight, but very strong; birds do not have teeth

Wing bones— hollow but strong

Sternum (keel)—powerful flight muscles are attached here

Leg bones—hollow, which means less weight to carry while flying

BIRDS' WINGS

A bird's wings are slightly curved from front to back. This gives the wing an **airfoil** shape that pulls the bird upwards through the air (**lift**)..

Because of the curved shape of a bird's wings, air flows over the top of the wing faster than it flows underneath. This produces lift.

The fast-moving air makes a low-pressure area on the top of the wing. A high-pressure area is made by the slower-moving air underneath the wings.

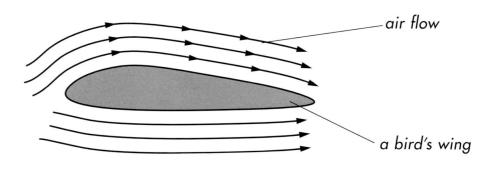

air flow

a bird's wing

With its sleek shape, the swallow can fly at speeds of up to 150 kilometers (93 miles) per hour.

A bird's wings have joints like elbows. The joints allow the wings to bend in the middle on the upstroke and straighten on the downstroke.

How a bird's wings move

On the downstroke, flight feathers close together. The air is pushed down and back, pulling the bird up and forwards through the air.

On the upstroke, wing feathers are opened to help the air pass through.

HOW BIRDS FLY

A bird's streamlined shape, strong yet light bones, and powerful flight muscles help it to fly. Birds use their wings to hold themselves in the air and move through it. Four forces act on birds when they fly: weight, lift, drag and **thrust**.

GLIDING AND SOARING

Many large birds such as albatrosses soar and glide in the air, which saves a great deal of energy. Gliding is flying without flapping the wings—without any forward propulsion.

Soaring is when a bird gains height by using rising air. Land birds such as buzzards and eagles can soar on **thermals** of warm rising air. They can circle within a thermal and rise effortlessly to many hundreds of feet without flapping their wings.

Lift is the force that pushes upward. It is caused by the movement of air over and under the wings

Drag is the force caused by air flowing past a bird and slowing it down

WANDERING ALBATROSS

The wandering albatross lives over the Southern Ocean. It glides and soars over the ocean for hours on its long slender wings. The wandering albatross depends on rising air currents to keep it in the air. It hardly ever needs to flap its wings.

Thrust is the force that moves a bird forward. A bird creates thrust by flapping its wings, which pushes the air behind it

Weight pulls the bird down. Two important things help keep a bird's weight low, their feathers and bones

A violet-eared hummingbird.

Hovering

Hovering is the process of keeping still in the air by beating the wings rapidly. Kestrels hover over the ground as they use their keen eyesight to search for prey.

Hummingbirds are the smallest flying birds. When they hover while feeding, their wings beat very quickly, over 100 beats per second.

FEATHERS

A bird's body is covered with soft, light, flexible feathers. Feathers are made of keratin, like our fingernails. A bird has two main types of feathers. These are contour feathers and down. Contour feathers cover the bird. They give it a smooth surface for flight and keep it waterproof. Down is usually under the contour feathers. It traps a layer of air to provide insulation.

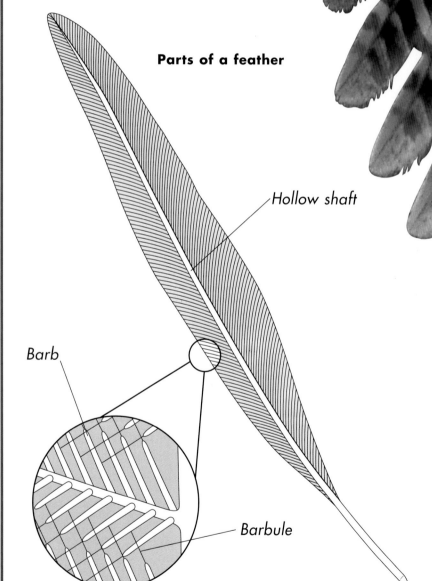

Parts of a feather

Hollow shaft

Barb

Barbule

A feather consists of a central hollow shaft. Barbs and barbules on each side of the shaft interlock and hook together to give the feather a smooth surface.

An eastern screech owl in flight.

Feather care

Birds care for their feathers when they preen. They use their beaks like a comb to zip their feathers' barbs and barbules together. They also oil their feathers when they are preening. Birds bathe often in water and dust.

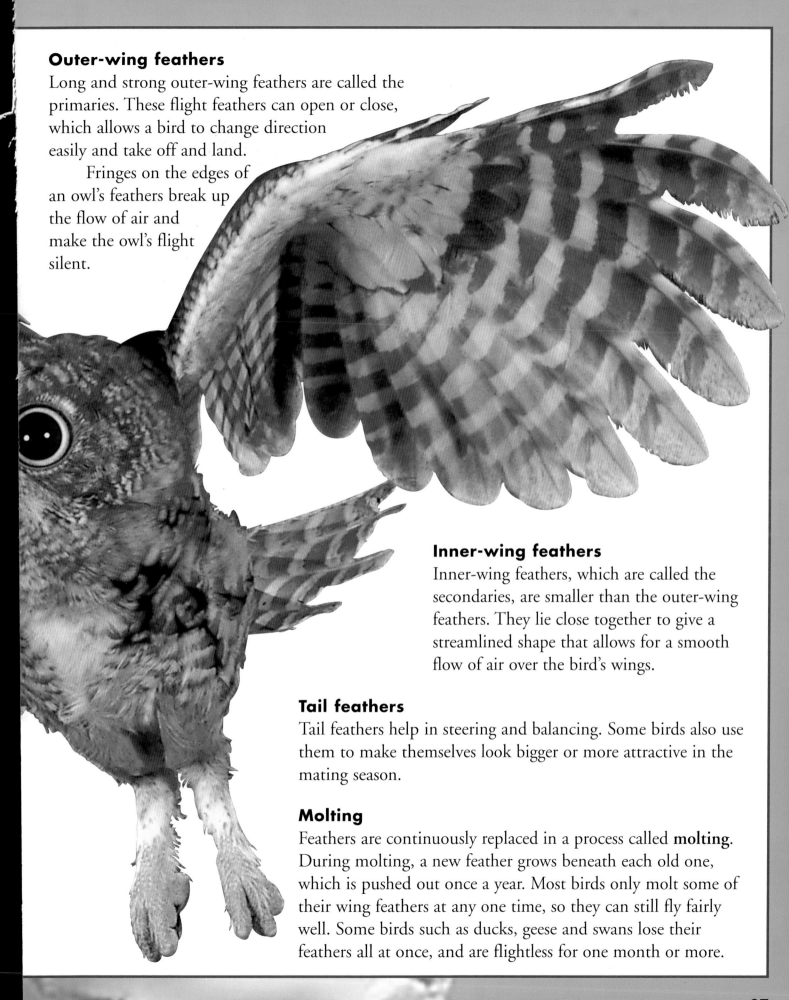

Outer-wing feathers

Long and strong outer-wing feathers are called the primaries. These flight feathers can open or close, which allows a bird to change direction easily and take off and land.

Fringes on the edges of an owl's feathers break up the flow of air and make the owl's flight silent.

Inner-wing feathers

Inner-wing feathers, which are called the secondaries, are smaller than the outer-wing feathers. They lie close together to give a streamlined shape that allows for a smooth flow of air over the bird's wings.

Tail feathers

Tail feathers help in steering and balancing. Some birds also use them to make themselves look bigger or more attractive in the mating season.

Molting

Feathers are continuously replaced in a process called **molting**. During molting, a new feather grows beneath each old one, which is pushed out once a year. Most birds only molt some of their wing feathers at any one time, so they can still fly fairly well. Some birds such as ducks, geese and swans lose their feathers all at once, and are flightless for one month or more.

27

WING SHAPES

A bird's wings are adapted to the life it lives. The shape and size of a bird's wings can show how a bird flies.

MIGRATION

Some birds migrate. They travel long distances in search of food, warmth and a place to breed and rear their young. Migratory birds can fly for thousands of miles. The most common **migration** of birds is the journey taken twice a year between winter and summer feeding grounds.

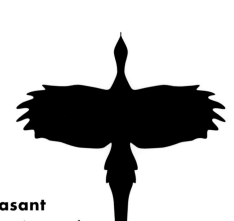

Vultures

Soaring birds such as vultures and eagles have long, broad wings with slotted wing tips for slow flying. Their wide wings assist them in rising on air currents.

Jays

Jays and other forest birds have short, wide wings to enable them to dodge in and out of trees.

Pheasant

Wide wings and a strong body give pheasants a powerful wing beat.

Swifts

Swifts catch insects in flight and have thin, swept-back wings for sustained flight at high speed.

Fulmars

Gliding birds such as fulmars and seagulls have long, thin wings for long-distance flying.

An African white-backed vulture.

Geese
Many geese travel enormous distances to breed. They fly steadily for many hours without stopping. They need long stretches of water for take-off or landing because of their long wings.

European swallows
The European swallow flies from northern Europe to South Africa and back again each year. This journey is 11,200 kilometers (6,960 miles) long.

The longest migration
The Arctic tern flies the longest journey of any bird. Each year it migrates from the Arctic to the Antarctic and back, a return journey of about 40,000 kilometers (24,856 miles).

The arctic tern spends eight months of every year in flight.

Fly like the birds

SINCE THE EARLIEST times, people have wanted to fly like the birds. Many people thought that if they strapped wings to themselves they would be able to fly.

LEONARDO DA VINCI (1452-1519)

In the fifteenth century, Leonardo da Vinci, the famous Italian artist and inventor, studied the flight of birds. He was the first to study flight scientifically and saw flight as a mathematical and mechanical problem.

Leonardo da Vinci's drawing of a man-powered ornithopter.

The ornithopter

Leonardo da Vinci sketched wing designs for 'ornithopters', which tried to copy the flapping wing movement of a bird's flight.

The 'ornithopter' was Leonardo da Vinci's design for a flapping wing machine that people would wear. Unfortunately, he never considered the shape of a bird's wings.

Machines were never made from any of da Vinci's designs. They would never have flown because they were too heavy. The ornithopter would have required enormous muscular energy to work, much more energy than a human could provide.

Glossary

agility	ability to maneuver quickly and effortlessly
airfoil	a shape with a curved surface designed to create lift in flight
articulated	having joints so bending is easy
cross-bracing	means of making a structure more rigid
evolution	the gradual change of a species from a simple to a more complex form
lift	the force that raises a bird or aircraft off the ground and keeps it in the air
metamorphosis	the changes in some insects as they grow. Their bodies undergo a complete change in shape
migration	the movement of a population of birds
molts	process of shedding old feathers
navigation	technique of arriving accurately at a desired destination
pupa	a central stage in the metamorphosis of an insect. The pupa looks like a small sack, and the insect develops into an adult inside it
roosts	places where animals sleep or rest
species	one kind of living thing that is so different from all other living things that it can breed only with others of its own kind. Each species has an individual scientific name
thermal	the rising current of air that allows birds to get lift
thrust	something that pushes forward
wingspan	the distance between wing tips when the wings are spread out

Index